LIST BUILDING TECHNIQUES FOR INTERNET MARKETERS

HOW TO GENERATE TARGETED SUBSCRIBERS IN ANY NICHE

ANTHONY EKANEM

Made with ♥ on the Notion Press Platform
www.notionpress.com

Contents

Preface

Before revealing the secrets of the trades, here are myths and fallacies that need to be

cleared before one indulges in building an opt-in list. These marketing misconceptions could pose so much of an obstacle towards your profiting well from your business.

Email marketing is one of the most effective marketing methods nowadays simply because virtually almost all people use email. Check on those email fields or blanks required to be filled up on various forms needed in processing different transactions. A person without an email address is tantamount to a person without an online home, which is one big shameful truth for this generation.

The not-so-secret way to surmount this dilemma is through permission-based advertising. There's no harm in trying after asking for permission. The key to this predicament is to have a very discerning eye on whom to email and whom to not email. Better look for some metrics on how to know which group of people would give you a high return on investment.

After clearing the fog regarding email marketing myths, here's how one can benefit from employing the power of email marketing campaigns - building an opt-in list. However, building an opt-in list is not a piece of cake, particularly for the uninitiated. Here is a rundown of tips on how to succeed in this kind of marketing endeavour.

Know which information from your audiences will help you in lowering expenses and/or making sales flourish. Devise a tactic to make people voluntarily provide you with the information necessary to create higher conversion.

An overload of data is not good. Ask only for opt-in, with their full name and email addresses. Make sure that the profiles that you gather are updated to aid in improving the relevance, timeliness and satisfaction of each deal you make.

An adage says it all, "*action speaks louder than words*". This easily translates to the difficulty one has to undergo during the execution of his or her email marketing efforts. It's a good thing that various methods, often low-cost, abound to hasten and facilitate the building up of one's opt-in database.

Tracking your email marketing results can pose great hardship, too. Technology and relevant sources should be employed in making this aspect of your marketing a lot more manageable. Your high-traffic groups of opt-ins with the greatest result should be taken note of.

The following are the most widely used methods to leverage channels without overspending:

1. Websites

It is an excellent tool for data collation and providing you with relevant information regarding your email offers. Use forms that solicit your visitor's email address and consent.

2. Print Ads, Brochures, TV, Radio

These are the more popular ways of marketing aiming to lead traffic to one's site.

You may want to ask for signups for email services. Make your website more visible through these media. Offering free electronic newsletters and/or rewards programmes can do well in making it easy to win the nod of your audiences, too.

3. Your Sales Force

Customer service associates can help a lot in making you benefit more from your email correspondence. Salespeople with proper education on how to aid you in this endeavour can very well contribute to higher ROI. Techniques like offering account updates and special programmes through email can easily land you those lists of valuable visitors.

4. Your Point of Sale

Forms for signup located at cash registers and other high-traffic and highly visible spots can be very excellent venues for your business to collect email addresses. Notification of upcoming sales through their email addresses and names can coax them to supply you with the information you need.

5. Conferences or trade shows

These tactics should be applied with adequate caution and should focus on earning the trust of your opt-in list instead of simply collating data for your sole own benefit. Always make sure that the forms that you will use and other methods that you will employ will not necessitate too much fuss to subscribe. This is for people to not be annoyed during the process of data supplication. With that bunch of information, who can ever go wrong with the feat of building an opt-in list?

CHAPTER ONE

Utilizing the Secrets of Opt-in Mailing Lists

Emails are replacing regular mail from the post office. Not only because it is *cheaper* since you do not need to buy a stamp, but it's also definitely faster. Emails can be sent in as fast as five seconds, depending on the server, anywhere in the world. No doubt, emails are being used to distribute newsletters, promotional emails, and other stuff. How then would you be able to round up email addresses to send those marketing

emails you have? Here is where an opt-in list comes in.

An opt-in list is a directory of email addresses you can send those emails to. Though it seems to be easy to find email addresses, if you are talking thousands in numbers, it is going to be hard. Besides, you must determine the recipient of the email. You wouldn't want your readers mostly male if you are selling lipsticks, right? A good opt-in list should include the profile of the email address owner. Here are tips on how to create a comprehensive opt-in list for a target market.

Create your website.

Creating a website is made simple nowadays. A lot of programmes are milling about assisting regular computer users in making and maintaining websites in a really simple way. Some website creators just need you to cut and paste, like a regular paint programme. Several web hosting sites are available too. Some are even free. If you have a site of your own, you can ask visitors to register with you or sign your guest book as they leave.

Set up a promotion or a freebie.

Not all the best things in life are free, as they say. But you can try to give something out for sure. You can see this done all over the web. *Free screensavers, free games, free download of programmes.* And what do they need from you? They just ask for an email address, your name and a little something more about you. Then you can place a check box on the registration form for sending of email. For sure, you can think of something to give out as well.

Write and write some more.

There are some web magazines where readers can submit their writings for a particular topic. If you had a chance to do so, add a link to your article providing information about what you are trying to promote. Some readers of your article may enjoy your work so much they'd like to contact you, so don't forget to leave your email address too.

Pose an easy opt-out option.

People who like to join your opt-in list would, along the way may want to opt out of it somehow. People who are wary of joining may not join at all if they see that it would be near impossible to remove their email addresses from the listing. Show them that it is as easy to opt out as it is to opt in.

Check other's strategies too.

It would be better if you can find a partner in generating an opt-in list. This way, you can split the expenses and both of you can share the list generated. It will be best to partner with a company that has a business like your line. Both of you can profit more should that be the case.

Use offline ways too.

You can put up a small raffle preferably in a supermarket for a certain item they buy. You can place an email address opt-in part in the raffle entry to add to your list. This way, you'd also know the buying preferences of the participants if you mark the entries systemically.

Creating an opt-in list entails a lot of work and funds. You should outline how much you will spend in creating an opt-in list. People appearing on opt-in lists are sales prospects.

They are those interested in a certain product that you may be selling. Obtaining an optimal opt-in list would boost your sales so these tools are undoubtedly essential. Acquire an opt-in list now or generate one. Either way, you are reaching people that can be your treasured customers for a long time!

CHAPTER TWO

What You Need to Do to Build Your List

Online marketing may have developed a sudden surge these past few years, but many in the know-how have felt its rise even from way then. As more Internet-based businesses are put up, the need to develop new marketing skills and knowledge based on this new medium has arisen. More and more marketing strategies are being discovered and developed to cope with the changing face of the business world.

The demand for online marketing tips and strategies has drastically grown and a new form of business has been born, Internet marketing strategies. While there are companies that are all too eager to help your site and business build a clientele for a fee, there are also many ways that can spread the word about your site's subsistence in a more cost-free way. One of these is Opt-in email marketing, also known as permission marketing.

Opt-in marketing requires the permission of a willing customer to subscribe to your marketing materials; materials that take the form of newsletters, catalogues and promotional mailings via e-mail. The more opt-in marketing mail is sent, the more chances there are to bag sales and more sales. To do this, you must build a list of all those who want to subscribe to your opt-in marketing list. From your list, you will get your targeted customers, this is a good list since they already have shown interest in what you must show and sell since they have willingly signed in for your list. These are the people who have liked what they have seen on your site and have decided they want to see more and maybe even purchase whatever product or service your company and site has to offer.

Many people would think that building their lists would take hard work and a lot of time to build and collect names and addresses. This is not so, it takes a bit of patience and some strategies but in doing this list, you open your site and your business to a whole new world of a target market. Make the effort to take your business to a new level, if traffic increase and good profits are what you want, an opt-in list will do wonders for your business venture.

There are many sources and articles on the Internet available for everyone to read and follow in building a list. Sometimes they may be confusing because there are so many and there are different ways. Different groups of people would have different approaches to building an opt-in list, but no matter how diverse many methods are, there are always some crucial things to do to build your list. Here are four of them.

1) Put up a good web form on your site that immediately follows the end of your content.

While some may say this is too soon to subscribe for a website visitors application, try to remember that your homepage should provide a quick good impression. If somehow a website visitor finds something that he or she doesn't like and turns them off, they may just forget about signing up.

A good web form for subscribing to an opt-in list is not hard to do. Just write a simple short statement about how they would like to see more and get updated about the site. Then there should be an area where they could put in their names and e-mail address. This web form will automatically save and send you the data inputted. As more people sign in, your list will be growing.

2) As mentioned in the first tip, make your homepage very, very impressive.

You need to have well-written articles and descriptions of your site. Depending on what your site is all about, you need to capture your website visitor's fancy. Make your site useful and very easy to use. Do not expect everyone to be tech-savvy. Invest in having good programming on your site and make your graphics beautiful but don't overdo it.

Don't waste your time making the homepage too overly large megabyte-wise. Not all people have dedicated T1 connections, the faster your site gets loaded, the better. Go for a look that borders between simplicity and sophisticated knowledge.

3) Provide good service and products.

A return customer is more likely to bring in more business. Even then and now, a satisfied customer will recommend a business always. Word of mouth and recommendations alone can rake in more business than an expensive ad. As your clientele roster grows so shall your list. With more members on the list, more people will get to know about what you have new to offer.

4) Keep a clean and private list.

If you provide emails to others and they get spammed, many will probably unsubscribe from you. Remember, a good reputation will drive more traffic and subscribers as well as strengthen the loyalty of your customers.

CHAPTER THREE

Quick and Easy Ways to Build a Profitable Opt-In List

Here I will offer more advice, for those who have started an opt-in list and have failed, you can rejuvenate your failed venture. For those who are starting, here are quick and easy ways to build a profitable opt-in list:

1) Get your customers to trust you and your products first.

Just launching your opt-in list would not make you an expert and a believable seller. Put many articles first before you start an opt-in list. Write about the topic you know and have started and used for your site. Try to put forums first to gain knowledge about your customers about their wants and needs and target those wants and needs.

Join forums from other sites as well. Provide expert advice and recommendations. When you feel that people trust you already, you will be able to start your opt-in list. You can build a base as well with other forum users. You can ask them to join your list. Friends are always good customers. Put up a link to your site so that they may be able to see what you're business is all about.

The certain truth is, the money will only come in when the consumers and subscribers believe and trust in you. They want a product or service that could be a good exchange for their money. People are not going to buy something out of your recommendation if they don't know you.

2) Find a product or service that people want and need.

Although it may not be your forte, if you provide a service and product that you have researched and learned about well, you can carry it forward. Invest your time, effort and money that you could sell as well as the buyers or subscribers of your opt-in list can use. While it is true that it is best to sell something that you have an interest in, there are not many people who have the same interest as you if you decide to sell something that is not entirely popular or profitable. Do your research well and you would see the profits come in. Also, provide your subscribers with promotional material that they could use and spread around.

3) Make friends with other opt-in list users.

This is beneficial especially if it is someone who has already launched a successful opt-in list. These are people that have experience in this venture and experience is still the best teacher. While there are many articles available for you on the Internet to use, there is nothing like getting a firsthand account from someone you trust.

Experienced opt-in list users will be able to tell you what to do and what not to do because they have gone through it. While different situations occur for different people, the general concept can still be very helpful. There are many things to avoid, and these people will be able to tell you which ones.

Important: Building a profitable opt-in list doesn't just happen *overnight*. There are many preparations and efforts to do. Opt-in lists are built from *scratch*, as your list grows, you should also maintain the quality of the list. Keep it organized and manageable. Get or hire help if need be, just make sure that your subscribers are happy and satisfied and they will be willing to buy from you.

CHAPTER FOUR

How to Get Your Opt-In Subscribers to Trust You Quickly

While the rest of the world has developed many barriers and protections to keep their e-mail accounts spam-free, some subscribe to emails that promote their products, services, and website. This is mainly because these subscribers want to know more about what these sites are offering and can be beneficial for them. They expect to be kept posted on what they are interested in and what is new in the market or field they have chosen.

Businesses would be so lucky to have these kinds of customers. The basic element needed to get these types of people is trust. When your customers trust you, they will reward you with their loyalty. Many Internet users have gone to great lengths in protecting their email accounts from spam mail. Some free-mail Internet providers and Internet service providers offer spam protection while some Internet-based companies screen your emails for you.

With an opt-in mail list, the emails you send containing your promotional materials such as newsletters, catalogues and marketing media will go through. Your intended recipient will be able to read and view what you have sent making it a successful transfer of information. To be able to be allowed to do so, you will need permission from your recipient, to get this permission; you need to be able to get their trust. With the great lack of disregard for privacy on the Internet, getting the trust of an internet user you don't personally know is a big achievement.

To build a good opt-in list you need people to trust you, for a faster and quicker build-up, you need to get your opt-in subscribers to trust you quickly. The faster you build your opt-in list the faster word about your site and the company gets to be spread. The bigger the scope of your opt-in list the more traffic you get spelling more profits. It is easy math if you think about it. Getting the numbers is not that simple though.

Getting the trust of your clientele shouldn't be so hard especially if you do have a legitimate business.

Getting your customers' trust should be based on your expertise. People rely on other people who know what they are talking about. Garner all the knowledge and information about your business. Well, frankly if you decide to go into a business most probably you have an interest in it. Like how many basketball payers become coaches, you don't venture into something you don't have any interest in.

Show your clients that you know what you are talking about.

Provide them with helpful hints and guidelines that pertain to what you are selling. Talk about how to install a roof if you are into hardware products or provide articles on insurance settlements if you're a settlement lawyer. You don't have to be a big corporation to make use of an opt-in list. If your customers see you as someone who knows what he is doing and saying, they will trust you quickly.

Be true to your customers, if you want to hype up your products and services, provide guarantees. The more satisfied customers you get, the bigger probability there is that they will recommend you. Generally, people will trust someone they know, when that someone recommends you then you're a shoo-in. They will go to your site and check it for themselves and be given a chance to experience what the other shave experienced from you, so make sure to be consistent in the service you provide.

Another tip for getting a customer to trust you quickly is to provide them with an escape hatch. Show them that you are not there to trap them. Keep a clean list that would enable them to unsubscribe anytime they want. Elaborate your web form by providing information on how to unsubscribe from the list. Guarantee them that they can let go of the service whenever they want to. Many are wary that they may be stuck for life and would have to abandon their email accounts when they get pestered with spam.

Remember that when you get the trust of your clients don't lose that trust. Because if you do anything with their email addresses like sell them or give them out, you will lose many members of your list as well as potential members. The true quickest way to gain the trust of your subscribers is when you are recommended by someone they trust.

CHAPTER FIVE

How to Make Money Using Your List

The more responsive subscribers you have, the more money you can make. Here are seven ways to make money using nothing more than your list.

1) Place advertisements.

Many corporations will be willing to pay to put their banners and ads on a list with many subscribers. Selling or renting out lists is not a good idea so rather than doing that, many companies would just rather place ads with lists that have a huge subscriber base. Your newsletter could be placed with many ads and each one spells money.

2) Have affiliations with other companies that have at least a semblance or relation

to what your site is about.

Here other companies will provide links and brief descriptions of what they offer, products and services. With every click made on the link that directs or leads a subscriber from your list to their site, the company will pay you.

3) Make deals with other companies by asking for a small percentage of sales done through your list.

With every sale done by customers that have come from your list and have gone there because of your newsletter, the other company will pay you a small percentage of your sales. The more people who buy from them, the more earnings you get.

4) You may also get products from other sites on a consignment basis and sell them to your list via your newsletter.

Place descriptions, articles and photos of the product in your newsletter. There will be those who will buy from you and when that happens, you can order the product from the other site and sell it to your buyer.

5) Sell e-books or a compilation of the articles on your list.

Manuals and how-to articles are in great demand. Many people will be willing to shell out money to gain knowledge about a certain topic and subject. With your existing list trusting your expertise in that area, an e-book could be offered and sold or used as an incentive.

6) Create a network out of your list.

Get people to invite more people to view your site and subscribe to your list. The larger your list is, the more people will be able to click on your links and affiliate links as well as make your advertisement rates higher.

7) Subscribers are willing to pay for information if they know that it can be trusted and relied upon.

Use your list to get more and more people to subscribe to you as well as browse your site. Lastly, you can use your list to earn money by making them your partners. Your list will be the bloodline of your growth and increase.

CHAPTER SIX

What to Avoid When Emailing Your List

While there are so many ways you can make people subscribe to your list, there are also some things you must do to avoid subscribers from wanting to get off your list. Aside from that, you also want to avoid any problems with the law and your Internet service provider. There are now many laws and rules that are applied to help protect the privacy of Internet users from spamming and unwanted mail. With the popularity of electronic mail as a medium for marketing because of the low cost, many companies have seized the opportunity and have flooded many people's e-mail accounts with promotional mail.

But, with an opt-in list, you avoid this annoyance because people subscribe to the list; they want to receive newsletters and promotional materials. They have consented to be on the list by subscribing themselves, just don't forget to put an unsubscribe feature every time in your opt-in list so that you avoid any confusion. There may be times when an email account was provided when the real owner didn't want to subscribe.

You must keep your list clean and manageable. Arrange it by using the many tools and technologies available for your opt-in list. Do not worry; your investment in this marketing strategy is well worth it with all the coverage you will get which will likely be converted into sales and then to profit.

Keep yourself and your business out of trouble and potential run-ins with the law and the internet service providers. Keep your operation legit and clean. Your reputation as a legitimate businessman and a legitimate site depends on your being a straight and true marketing strategist. As a tip, here are three things to avoid when emailing your list.

1) Take notice of your unsuccessful sends.

These are the e-mails that bounce. Bounced emails, also known as undeliverable messages, are those messages that, for whatever reason, were not successfully received by the intended recipient. Some bounces happen or occur because the server was busy at that time but can still be delivered at another time. There are also bounces because the inbox of the recipient is full at that time. There are those bounce messages that are simply undeliverable ever. The reason for this is that it may be an invalid email address, a misspelt email address, or an email address that was abandoned and erased already.

Manage your list by putting markings on those that bounce. Erase an email account from your list so that you have accurate statistics and records as to how many are receiving your mail. You may also want to check the spelling of the email addresses in your list. One common mistake is when an N instead of an M is placed in the .com area.

2) Always provide an unsubscribe feature on your site and an unsubscribe link in your emails.

When someone in your list files a request to be unsubscribed, always take that request seriously. If you don't take them off your list and keep sending them your e-mails, you are now sending them spam mail. When you are reported as a spammer, you and your business can get into a lot of trouble. You can be reported to the authorities and maybe blacklisted by many internet service providers. You will lose a lot of subscribers this way and many more potential subscribers.

3) Do not provide pornographic or shocking and disturbing content in your newsletters.

It is hard to decipher the age of the recipient and many complaints may stem from this. Controversial issues also are to be avoided to not be branded by your subscribers. Stick to the nature of your site and business. Always remember these tips in this article so that you can have a healthy relationship with your subscribers as well as be kept within the boundaries of what is allowed in sending mails to an opt-in list.

CHAPTER SEVEN

How to Build a List of Eager Subscribers

Every online business provides great service to generate satisfaction among its customers. As every customer receives satisfaction over their products or the services they get, there is a great chance that they will become a return customer and buy again. Better yet, they will recommend you to other people that could generate more business for you and your site.

As more traffic is driven to your site, you can entice many of them to subscribe to your mailing list or opt-in list. This is a list where website visitors agree to be sent promotional materials such as newsletters, catalogues and such that could keep them updated about your site or the niche of your site. These promotional materials are sent via e-mail to the members of the list at different time intervals.

When using e-mail as the media of your marketing and advertisements, you eliminate the need for high costs. Email is free and if you can manage to make your promotional advertisements you can also save a bundle there. With an opt-in subscribers list, you are pretty sure that what you are sending out is received, viewed, and read by the subscribers and not simply deleted. They have signed up for service and have consented to receive it.

This means that there are constant reminders to your subscribers about all your products, new products, and services as well as any promotions and special deals you are having. There is also the chance that they can be forwarded to other potential customers as they tell their friends and families about you and your site.

Of course, you should be also aware that a subscriber may *unsubscribe* when they feel that they are not getting what they want or expected. Make sure that they are satisfied with your opt-in marketing strategies and keep them excited about receiving your newsletters and catalogues. Here are some tips that can help you build a list of eager subscribers.

Make your promotional materials interesting and fun. Try to use a little creativity but not too over-artsy. Build around what your product or service is about. For example; if you are selling car parts, put some pictures of what is new in the auto parts world, a new wing door possibly that can fit any car and make it look like a Lamborghini.

Try to research what people are looking for, this way, you stay one step ahead of them all the time and you will be their bearer of new tidings. They will be eager to receive what you are sending them because they know you always have fresh and new things to share with them.

Write good articles that can be very informational but the light at the same time. If your subscribers enjoy your articles, they will go to your site by clicking the links that you will be putting on your newsletter to read some more. You can provide articles that can connect to many people. Be diverse in your articles. Put something humorous, then put something informational, then put something that has both.

Are you wary about this because you don't like writing? No problem, many professional and experienced article writers can do the job for you for minimal fees. They know what they are doing and can provide the need that you have for your newsletters, the money that you pay for your articles is going to be met by the many sign-ups and the potential profit from the sales that you will get.

Create and send an eBook to your customers about anything related to your business or site. Use your knowledge and expertise in the field you have chosen to help other people who are similarly interested. Offer this e-book for free. You can write about anything informational and helpful to your subscribers. For example, you can do manuals and guides on so many things. This e-book could be used as a reference for many people.

Share this e-book with everyone, even other sites; just make sure that they don't change the links in the e-book that will lead people to your site. If you want, you can always get some people to write it for you just like your articles. Your investment once again will be covered by the great marketing this will generate.

Add e-coupons in your newsletters that will help them avail of special discounts. Put a control number in your e-coupon so that it can only be used once. When people get discounts that can be found in your newsletters, they will be eager to receive your newsletter in anticipation of what you are promoting next. If your subscribers can get benefits from your newsletters, they will be very eager to receive them. Just don't flood your mailing list with emails so that you don't annoy your subscribers.

In Closing... And a Call to Action!

As the book enters the wrap-up in this chapter, I will share with you something valuable. If you aim for success, you must do everything within your means to achieve that. You just don't go on sitting there in your house complaining about not getting as much profit as you expect. You must keep moving. You must pour in and invest enough time, money and effort to have profitable results. In doing Internet business, you must aim just the same. You should maximize all your Internet marketing strategies, given the wide market that your business will be exposed to. Imagine the whole online community as potential clients!

Now, one of the best marketing tools that you can use in your online business is building a list (which is the subject of this book!). An opt-in list is the best, most effective and smartest option that you can make to make it big. It is one thing to stay in business and it is another thing to have a profitable business.

So, if you will be allowed to choose, make use of the building list to ensure that profits will keep coming in. And building a list will work for your benefit. This will ensure that you can maintain close contact and a good relationship with your clients, especially frequent visitors.

This will also save you money, time and effort because once you come up with a new product or new information, you know exactly to whom you will send updates. After all, you have a definite market.

This is one aspect that you will have to maintain to have a steady source of income at the least. Then the rest of your efforts will be to make the number of your regular clients grow.

Some pointers for building your opt-in list:

1. You should put a 'subscribe link' or 'subscribe box' on your website. It is advisable to put it on all the pages. Then make sure that it is strategically positioned,

meaning it has to be easily located by the visitors. The upper right-hand corner of the page would be a good position.

1. Promote your website and promote it even more, to make give it more exposure and to get more subscribers.

3. Come up with contests or give away freebies and goodies that will require visitors to give out their email ads to be able to join.

4. Give out information, articles, and updates to your clients with your links in them. Make sure that the information will be relevant to the client.

5. Offer free courses to your visitors. This will also help maintain a good relationship with your subscribers.

6. Use your signature also to make your opt-in list expand. Every time you send out messages the link information should be included.

7. Do some networking too. Join some forums or discussions and build relationships with the people there. This way will also be a good way for you to get more contacts and clients. At the same time, you should also know what you should avoid in building an opt-in list. There is one thing that you should keep in mind as the *don'ts* of building a list.

8. Never spam your subscribers. You should get permission from your subscribers, or else you might end up with a bad reputation.

9. Avoid abrasive pop-ups (though not all). They can sometimes annoy visitors. There are also pop-up blockers now. Your effort here might end up futile. You should also refrain from flooding your subscribers with information. You might end up annoyed that you might not get a favourable result. There may be times that you'll give relevant information, but your clients may just dismiss it. The benefits of having many regular subscribers are undeniable. They will keep your business going and you will enjoy the profits that will come in. Just remember that things don't end there.

10. Once you've built up a substantial opt-in list, make sure that you maintain it well. Keep in contact with your subscribers. Send them updates. Give out special offers and helpful tips. Freebies will be helpful too.

9 798889 860426

Printed by Libri Plureos GmbH in Hamburg, Germany